Rodale's *High Health* Cookbook Series

THE
GOOD GRAINS

Rodale's *High Health* Cookbook Series

THE
GOOD GRAINS

by the Editors of Rodale Books

Series Editorial Director:
Charles Gerras

Text Preparation:
Camille Cusumano
Carol Munson

Recipe Research and Editing:
Camille Bucci

Illustrations:
Jean Gardner

Art Director:
Karen A. Schell

Series Designer:
Jerry O'Brien

Copy Editing:
Jan Barckley

Cover Photography:
Carl Doney

Food Stylist:
Laura Hendry Reifsnyder

Rodale Press, Emmaus, Pennsylvania

Printed in the United States of America on recycled paper, containing a high percentage of de-inked fiber.

The recipes in this book have appeared in other Rodale publications.

Library of Congress Cataloging in Publication Data
Main entry under title:

The Good grains.

(Rodale's high health cookbook series ; v. 2) Includes index.
1. Cookery (Cereals) 2. Cereals as food. I. Rodale Books. II. Series.
TX808.G66   641.6′31   81-21048
ISBN 0-87857-391-7   hardcover   AACR2

2 4 6 8 10 9 7 5 3 1   hardcover

Contents

Getting Back to the Good Grains

*T*he joy all men once took in the gift of whole grains is having a long-overdue renaissance in America. Suddenly we are aware again of the wide variety of grains available to us, and we see them as a source of limitless, low-cost nutrition and eating pleasure in an era of high-priced food.

Our ancient ancestors, grateful to have them as a reliable buffer against starvation, worshipped the common grains as gods. The Babylonians venerated wheat; to the Chinese, rice was the source and sustainer of life; the Incas celebrated corn as a child of the sun, a deity, a life source on earth.

Grains held this place of high esteem because the ancient peoples saw grains as a source of nourishing plentitude. Today we understand how right they were! We know now that many whole grains are rich in the life-supporting essential amino acids. They also contain significant amounts of the mineral iron and the B vitamins thiamine, riboflavin, and niacin—nutrients useful as a defense against pellagra, anemia, and other deficiency diseases.

The Right Kind of Carbohydrates

Though grains are somewhat richer in calories than other staple foods, the calories come from complex carbohydrates, not from fats. So grains provide necessary carbohydrates, while minimizing whatever risks might be involved with excessive cholesterol in fatty foods. Since grains have been the major human food source for centuries, we know that man can live and thrive on a diet that consists primarily of these nutrition-rich high-carbohydrate foods. What makes it all work so well is that humans learned long ago to complement the grains with eggs, milk, cheese, bits of meat—foods that subtly supply nutrients that allow for the full use of the protein in grains.

Making whole grains a larger part of your diet is bound to increase your intake of precious trace minerals. Whole grains are an important source of chromium, manganese, copper, zinc, selenium, and magnesium—minerals that are vital to the body's life processes.

We know now that grains are most useful when processed in a primitive way—sprouted or ground into meal or flour—rather than milled and degermed, with the bran removed. Used in their unrefined state, grains not only provide relief from fat-rich meat and milk products, but they mean more fiber-rich protein. The role of fiber in our diet has been recognized as crucial in preventing many of the "diseases of civilization"—bowel disorders, heart disease, diabetes, obesity, ulcers, gallstones, and varicose veins. It follows that substituting grains for some of the meat in our diets can add more and better years to life.

It is hard for us to appreciate the central role grain played in the diets of primitive people—and still plays in the diets of some backward societies today. The wheat, the rice, and the corn were not the "starch" on a varied dinner menu; they were the dinner! People didn't use bread merely to accompany the main course; the bread was the main course. And when the early cultures of Latin America learned to make corn into patties, breads, and cakes, it was always the core of the meal. Anything else—fruit, vegetables, even meat—was an unimportant extra, a find, a flavoring.

It is a perfectly reasonable view. Grains work well as a fundamental base for all other foods. Serve just a little milk and fruit or vegetable with any of the staple grains and you have a subsistence diet. Simply adding a dairy product to any grain raises its protein value 25 percent.

The same wholesome, delicious, health-giving grain foods that have pleasured and nourished the world for thousands of years are all still available. You can try recipes for some of the most nutritious and appealing grain dishes ever created when you become better acquainted with the following popular grains.

HOW TO HANDLE WHOLE GRAINS IN YOUR KITCHEN

When you decide to incorporate whole grains into your meal planning, you will most likely want to keep several of the different varieties on hand. While your neighborhood supermarket may carry brown rice and some of the more common grains, a natural foods store is the best source for a wider variety of organically grown whole grains. If cooking with whole grains is new to you, buy small amounts at first. When you are ready to stock up, be sure you are familiar with these simple instructions for storing and preparing whole grains.

Storing Grains Properly

Unhulled grain with its nutritious germ intact has a higher oil content than refined grain, so proper storage is necessary to ward off rancidity, which ruins the flavor and cuts into the grain's nutritional value. Sealed in a tightly covered container, in a cool, dry place, most grains will keep for about a year. Buckwheat groats and oatmeal spoil more quickly, so they should be refrigerated or used within a month of purchase. Bulgur stores very well — the par-cooking it gets in production guards against rancidity. By the way, insects thrive on healthy grain, so use a well-closed container to protect your supply against infestation.

How to Cook Grains

All grains may be cooked according to a basic method that does not require much work at all. Cooked in a liquid until swollen and tender, the grains may then be prepared in any way desired. Millet and barley increase from three and a half to four times their original amount, while other grains swell two and a half to three times their size. Some grains such as rye, wheat, and triticale are so hard they may require a rather lengthy cooking period. To shorten this cooking time and cut down on energy use, soak these grains before cooking (see Grain Cooking Chart, p. 9). To decide how much grain to cook, refer to the grain's cooked volume given in the cooking chart. You should allow a half cup of cooked grain per person for breakfast or as a side dish, and one cup cooked grain for main-dish servings.

Basic Cooking Method

1. Rinse the raw grain well under cold water. This will help remove both surface grit and excess starch, as well as start the swelling process.

2. Bring correct amount of cooking liquid to a boil in a pot large enough to accommodate the increase in volume after cooking. Meat or vegetable stock, juice, milk, or water may be used. The more flavorful the cooking liquid, the more flavorful the cooked grains will be.

3. Add grain to the boiling liquid. Stir once.

4. Allow the liquid to return to boiling, then turn heat down to the lowest possible setting. Cover and cook grains slowly until they are soft and the cooking liquid has been absorbed. This will take anywhere from 15 minutes for bulgur to two hours for wheat berries and the harder grains.

To determine if the grain is cooked, use the taste test: Well-cooked grain will be chewy, but not tough or hard. If not quite done, add a little more water, cover, and continue cooking.

Grain Cooking Chart

Grain	Amount Uncooked (cups)	Amount of Water (cups)	Cooking Method and Time[1]	Amount of Cooked Grain (cups)
Barley	1	4	Boil – 30-40 minutes	4
Buckwheat	1	2-5[2]	Boil – 20 minutes	3
Bulgur	1	2	Boil – 15 minutes	2½
Cornmeal	1	4-5[3]	Boil or Double Boiler – 30-40 minutes	4-5
Millet	1	4	Boil or Double Boiler – 25-30 minutes	4
Oatmeal	1	2	Boil – 10 minutes	4
Rice (Brown)	1	2-2½[4]	Boil – 35-40 minutes	2½
Rye	1	4	Boil – 1 hour or more[5]	2⅔
Triticale	1	4	Boil – 1 hour or more[5]	2½
Wheat Berries	1	3½	Boil – 1 hour or more[5]	2½

Notes

1. All whole grains may be cooked by the thermos method. Place 1 cup grain in a quart thermos (preferably wide-mouth) and add boiling water almost to the top, leaving 1-inch headspace between water and stopper of thermos. Using a long wooden spoon handle, stir grain to distribute evenly. Close and leave for 8 to 12 hours. (For rice, add only 1½ cups boiling water and leave only 8 hours.)

Another method for cooking grains is the pilaf method. This involves sauteing the grain, usually with minced onion, in oil and then adding stock or water, approximately twice as much liquid as grain, and cooking it, covered, over medium-low heat until the liquid is absorbed and the grain is tender. The time is about the same as above. Brown rice, bulgur, barley, millet, and wild rice are especially good cooked this way.

(continued on next page)

The pressure cooker method offers the advantage of cutting the cooking time in the above chart in half. In general, use twice as much water as grain when cooking in the pressure cooker, although more water—4 times the amount of grain—is needed for the harder grains, such as rye, triticale, and wheat.

2. Buckwheat is traditionally cooked by the pilaf method, but a raw egg is usually stirred into the dry grains before adding the stock or water. This replaces the need for sauteing the buckwheat in oil and is done to keep the grains separate throughout the cooking. The required amount of water is 2 cups for the "egg" method of cooking buckwheat and 5 cups when cooking it to be eaten as a cereal.

3. The lesser amount of water is to be used when you wish to have a stiff cooked cornmeal, as for cornmeal mush.

4. The lesser amount of water is required for short- or medium-grain rice, the larger amount for long-grain rice.

5. The cooking time for these grains may be longer than 1 hour, depending on their age, where and how they were grown, and other unknown variables. It is best to taste test the grains after an hour of cooking. They will not be quite as tender as other grains when done, but will have a nice chewy texture.

Wheat, rye, and triticale may be brought to a boil in the required amount of water, boiled for 10 minutes, then left to soak for 8 to 12 hours in this same water. After the long soaking, they may be cooked for 15 to 20 minutes and will be tender enough to eat. This is one way to shorten the cooking time.

A Further Tip on Cooking Grains

To enhance the flavor and shorten cooking time, toast grains in a dry, medium-hot iron skillet, stirring constantly, until they have a pleasant fragrance and take on a darker color. This also enables the grain to be "cracked" or coarsely ground in an electric blender.

BARLEY

*A*mericans generally reserve barley for soup or beer-making, but barley has much greater possibilities worth exploring. It makes a delicious pilaf when cooked in chicken broth and mixed with onions and mushrooms. Many English women credit their fabled complexions to a drink made from the water barley cooks in. They and others also brew a hot drink (used as a coffee substitute in America) from roasted barley, sometimes mixed with other grains.

Barley is most readily available pearled, in which case it has had its nutritious outer husk removed by abrasion. Whole-grain brown barley (also known as pot or scotch), which is more difficult to find, has only a single outer layer removed and retains more nutrients. However, it must be soaked overnight before it is cooked.

Barley Water

Don't throw away the water drained from barley that has been cooked. Save it to drink, either as is or flavored with honey, fruit, or herbs to taste. Barley water is rich in nutrients, and it is used as an aid to healthy skin by English women who are famous for their glowing complexions.

To make barley water from scratch, simmer ¼ cup barley in 1¼ quarts water for about an hour. Squeeze 1 lemon and 2 or 3 oranges and set the juice aside. Pour off the water in which barley has been cooked, add the fruit rinds to it, and let cool. Then remove the rinds, add the fruit juice, and refrigerate for future use. It is a refreshing, healthful drink. The barley itself can be used for another dish.

Russian Barley Soup

½ cup barley

1 small onion, minced

1 tablespoon butter

2 cups chicken stock

¼ teaspoon dried dillweed

¼ teaspoon ground coriander

½ teaspoon dried mint

1 tablespoon rye or whole wheat flour

2 eggs, beaten

1 cup yogurt

2 tablespoons lemon juice

chopped parsley

chopped mint

Cook barley according to preferred method (see Index).

In a 5-quart soup pot, saute onion in butter. Heat chicken stock to boiling and stir onion and cooked barley, with any remaining liquid, into stock. Add herbs.

Blend flour into eggs, then carefully stir in yogurt. Add a little of the hot soup to the egg and yogurt mixture, gradually stirring it in to avoid "scrambling" the eggs, then pour this back into the hot soup. Stir in lemon juice. Keep hot but do not permit to boil. Add parsley and mint just before serving.

Serves 6 to 8

4 cups stock

¾ cup barley

½ cup dried or frozen green peas

1 small turnip

2 medium-large carrots

1 medium-size leek or onion

2 cups chopped kale

3 sprigs parsley

Scotch Broth

*P*lace stock in a 4-quart soup pot and bring to a boil. Wash barley and peas and add to stock.

Dice turnip. Cut up 1 carrot and grate the other. Add vegetables to stock and let soup simmer 45 minutes to 1 hour.

Serves 8

Pure Malted Barley Drink

For people who don't like the taste of chicory, or for those whose digestive systems do not react too well to it, there is the German drink *Kathreiners Malzkaffee.* This beverage is made from pure malted barley, roasted, nothing added. It is brewed like coffee and can be drunk with or without milk and sweetener. It is tasty and easy on the stomach. In Germany it is an accepted beverage for the whole family, especially for children. It is available in any grocery store handling imported foods, and in some natural foods stores.

Barley Saute Monterey

1 cup chopped onions

2 cloves garlic, chopped

2 tablespoons butter

1 tablespoon oil

4 cups cooked barley

1 small eggplant, cut into ½-inch cubes

2 small zucchini, sliced thick

1 teaspoon dried oregano

pinch of cayenne pepper

2 cups cooked tomatoes

¼ pound Monterey Jack or mozzarella cheese, grated

In a large heavy skillet, saute onions and garlic in butter-oil mixture. When translucent, add barley and saute 2 minutes longer.

Add eggplant and zucchini, stirring to coat the vegetables. Sprinkle on seasonings, saute 30 seconds to release flavors, then add tomatoes and simmer only until vegetables are barely tender.

Stir in cheese over very low heat until the cheese has melted; or top with cheese and melt it quickly under the broiler until bubbly.

Serves 4

1 tablespoon dry yeast

¼ cup lukewarm water

1 tablespoon honey

2 tablespoons butter

1¼ cups barley flour

¼ cup buttermilk

1 egg

Barley-Buttermilk Biscuits

Soften yeast in water, add honey, and allow mixture to set about 15 minutes, or until frothy.

With 2 knives or a pastry blender, cut butter into barley flour. Combine buttermilk and egg and beat slightly, then stir into the flour mixture. Add yeast mixture, mix thoroughly, and let the whole mixture stand 20 minutes.

Preheat oven to 400°F. Drop dough by the tablespoonful onto an oiled baking sheet. Pat into 2-inch rounds and bake 15 to 18 minutes, or until nicely browned.

Makes 1 dozen 2-inch biscuits

Barley-Oat Pie Crust

1 cup barley flour

1 cup oat flour

⅓ cup oil

6 tablespoons ice water

*P*reheat oven to 400°F.

Prepare a 9-inch pie pan by brushing bottom and sides lightly with oil.

Sift dry ingredients into a bowl.

Mix oil and ice water. Add liquid to dry ingredients, using a fork. Stir until a ball is formed.

Press into prepared pie pan, or roll out between wax paper and place in pie pan, making a high edge around the outside. Prick with fork and bake 10 to 12 minutes.

Makes 1 9-inch pie shell

Note: This crust can be made with whole wheat flour: Simply use 1½ cups whole wheat instead of the combination of barley and oat.

Basic Method for Making Lattice Top

Roll the pastry dough for the pie top into an oblong. Cut into strips ½ inch wide. Lay strips across the filling, parallel to each other approximately 1 inch apart. Turn the pie slightly, and instead of laying the top layer of strips perpendicular (or at right angles) to the bottom layer of strips, lay them diagonally (or on a slant). This gives the impression that the strips are woven. Lay a strip of pastry all around the rim of the pan, covering the ends of the lattice strips. Pinch this to make an attractive edge all round the pie.

4 teaspoons dry yeast

½ cup lukewarm water

1 to 2 tablespoons honey

2 eggs

⅓ cup soy milk powder

¼ cup skim milk powder

1 cup water

1 cup barley flour

2 tablespoons oil

1 cup wheat germ

Barley Pancakes

Sprinkle yeast over the surface of lukewarm water in a mixing bowl. Stir in honey and allow mixture to "work" in a warm place about 25 minutes.

Gradually blend in eggs. Combine soy milk powder and skim milk powder with 1 cup water, using a wire whisk, and add to yeast mixture. Then add barley flour, oil, and wheat germ.

Cook on a lightly greased griddle over medium heat (¼ cup batter for each pancake). When bubbles form on surface, turn pancake and cook about 2 minutes longer, or until nicely browned on underside.

Serves about 5

1 tablespoon dry yeast

½ cup lukewarm water

1 teaspoon honey

2 tablespoons sesame oil or other oil

2 cups barley flour

½ cup sesame seeds

4 cups whole wheat flour

3 cups hot water

2 tablespoons sesame oil or other oil

½ cup whole wheat flour

1 egg, beaten

1 teaspoon water

¼ cup sesame seeds

Tibetan "Prayer Wheel" Barley Bread

Sprinkle yeast over lukewarm water, add honey to mixture, and leave to "work" while preparing the dough.

Put 2 tablespoons oil in a heavy iron skillet and over medium-high heat brown barley flour and ½ cup sesame seeds, stirring constantly, until flour is an even tan color. Take care to prevent it from burning.

Remove mixture from skillet and put it into a large bowl. Stir in 4 cups whole wheat flour.

Mix hot water and 2 tablespoons oil and stir into flour mixture until ingredients are completely combined. Allow mixture to cool until it tests lukewarm to the wrist.

Tibetan "Prayer Wheel" Barley Bread—continued

When mixture is lukewarm, stir in the yeast mixture. Using ½ cup whole wheat flour, knead dough 15 minutes on a floured board, until it is smooth to the touch.

Place dough in a large oiled bowl and turn it over to oil the surface. Cover with a damp cloth and allow to rise in a warm, draft-free place overnight.

In the morning, carefully place on an oiled baking sheet, keeping the shape of the risen dough. Do not reknead, punch down, or reshape in any way.

Combine egg with water and brush top of dough with mixture. Sprinkle ¼ cup sesame seeds over surface.

With the tip of a sharp knife, score a large cross on the surface of the loaf. Allow the loaf to spread on baking sheet 1 hour in a warm, draft-free place.

Preheat oven to 450°F. After an hour, when the loaf will resemble a large wheel, bake 1 hour. The high temperature produces a crusty exterior and tender interior. Cool loaf on a rack before slicing.

Makes 1 large loaf

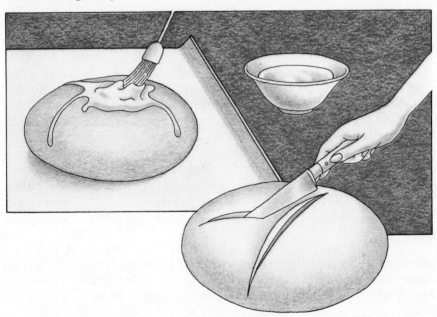

BUCKWHEAT

*I*n any place but Russia, a white field of buckwheat in full bloom is a rare sight. To Americans, buckwheat means pancakes. But in Russia, buckwheat gets the attention it deserves as a flavorful sustaining food and the basis for many traditional dishes. Every Russian cook is trained early in the art of preparing *kasha*. If times are good, the kasha is made into a kind of pilaf with meat stock and the addition of some fried onions and egg or a bit of meat. For centuries, the classic Russian meal has been kasha with cabbage, black bread, and sour cream. Another is *kasha varnitchkes*, made with kasha and noodles. The Russians also use buckwheat flour to make *blini*, those marvelous paper-thin crepes that are served hot, eight or ten at a time.

Wherever buckwheat is an important part of the cuisine, it is used mostly in the form of groats (hulled kernels, whole or crushed). Natural foods stores sell them roasted and unroasted. Some people buy both and mix them, half-and-half, to make an interesting base for a casserole.

½ cup buckwheat groats

2½ cups boiling water

⅓ cup raisins

Buckwheat Porridge

Stir groats into boiling water in a 2-quart saucepan and cook about 20 minutes, or until soft. Add raisins and cook 5 minutes longer. Sweeten with honey, if desired. Serve with milk.

Yields 3 cups

1½ to 2 pounds brisket of beef, or chuck

2 tablespoons oil

Buckwheat Cholent

1 large onion, finely chopped

1 cup navy beans

1 cup buckwheat groats

pinch of pepper

4 cups boiling water

*B*rown meat in oil in a Dutch oven or heavy soup pot with a tight-fitting lid. Add onion and saute until lightly browned. Keeping the meat in the center of the pot, add remaining ingredients. Cover and cook in a very slow oven (200°F) 8 hours or overnight. Serve with tomato sauce or catsup.

Serves 6 to 8

2½ cups milk

½ cup buckwheat groats

⅓ cup grated sharp Cheddar
   cheese

4 egg yolks, beaten

1½ teaspoons prepared mustard

1 tablespoon tamari soy sauce

4 egg whites

Buckwheat Groat Souffle

*H*eat milk in a medium-size saucepan. Add groats and bring to a boil, stirring constantly. Cover, lower heat, and simmer about 20 minutes. Add cheese and stir until cheese is melted. Remove from heat and gradually pour over egg yolks, stirring until well blended. Add mustard and tamari. Cool.

Preheat oven to 350°F. Beat egg whites until stiff and gently fold them into buckwheat mixture. Turn into an ungreased 1½-quart souffle dish. Bake 40 to 45 minutes, or until souffle is firm to the touch. Serve immediately.

Serves 4 to 6

Buckwheat-Stuffed Cabbage Rolls

1 medium-size onion, finely chopped

½ green pepper, finely chopped

3 tablespoons oil

2 cups buckwheat groats

4 cups boiling water

½ cup chopped peanuts

¼ cup chopped sunflower seeds

1 head cabbage

warm water

Saute onion and green pepper in oil until tender (about 5 minutes). Add groats and stir until coated with oil. Add boiling water, cover, and simmer 15 minutes, or until groats are tender and water has been absorbed. Add peanuts and sunflower seeds.

While groats are cooking, core cabbage and steam until leaves are pliable. Separate the leaves and place 2 heaping tablespoons of the groat mixture on each leaf. Roll up, tucking in the sides.

Preheat oven to 350°F. Place cabbage rolls in an oiled baking dish. Pour warm water over rolls to reach three-quarters of the way up the sides of the dish. Cover and bake 1½ hours, or until cabbage is tender.

Makes 16 cabbage rolls

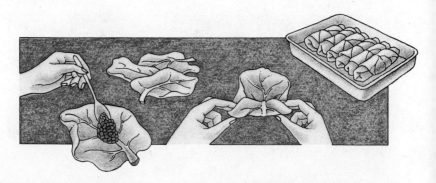

1 cup buckwheat groats

1 cup cottage cheese

3 egg yolks

1 tablespoon chopped parsley

1 teaspoon chopped chives

1 teaspoon dried basil

½ teaspoon dried thyme

3 egg whites

Cottage Cheese-Buckwheat Squares

Cook buckwheat according to preferred method (see Index). Drain if necessary.

Preheat oven to 400°F. Puree cottage cheese briefly in an electric blender until smooth. Add cooked groats and mix well. Beat egg yolks slightly and add to cheese-groat mixture. Add seasonings and mix thoroughly. Beat egg whites until stiff and fold into the mixture. Pour into a buttered rectangular baking pan and spread to about ½-inch thickness.

Bake about 30 minutes, or until top is brown. Cut into squares and serve as a side dish with meat or an all-vegetable dinner.

Serves 4

Buckwheat Blini

¼ cup skim milk powder

1 cup water

2 teaspoons dry yeast

4 egg yolks

1 teaspoon honey

4 tablespoons oil

1½ cups sifted buckwheat flour

4 egg whites

Combine skim milk powder with water, using a wire whisk. Heat over medium heat until bubbles form on sides of saucepan. Remove from heat and cool to lukewarm. Stir in yeast until softened.

In a mixing bowl, beat egg yolks until thick. Blend the yeast mixture into beaten yolks. Stir in honey and oil.

Gradually blend buckwheat flour into batter, mixing thoroughly.

Set bowl over a pan of warm water, cover, and let rise until doubled in bulk (about 1¼ hours).

Beat egg whites until soft peaks form when beater is raised. Fold gently but thoroughly into batter.

Preheat a lightly oiled griddle over medium heat until hot. Cook pancakes on griddle until bubbles form on edges and pancakes are golden brown; turn pancakes and cook 2 minutes longer. Lightly oil griddle periodically.

Makes 8 to 12 pancakes

½ cup buckwheat groats

¼ cup butter

⅓ cup molasses

½ teaspoon cinnamon

2 tablespoons dry yeast

3 tablespoons lukewarm water

1 tablespoon honey

1 cup buckwheat flour

1½ cups whole wheat flour

¼ cup wheat germ

⅔ cup warm water

Buckwheat Kasha Bread

Cook buckwheat groats according to preferred method (see Index). Drain if necessary.

Put cooked groats in a large mixing bowl. Add butter, molasses, and cinnamon. In a small bowl, soften yeast in lukewarm water, add honey, and set aside until frothy.

Combine the 2 mixtures, then add the flours, wheat germ, and warm water. Beat 3 minutes. Cover with a towel and put in a warm place to rise 1 hour.

Stir the dough down and put in a large oiled loaf pan. Let rise 1 hour.

Preheat oven to 400°F. Bake 15 minutes. Lower heat to 375°F and bake 55 minutes longer, or until done. Remove from pan and cool on a rack.

Makes 1 loaf

CORN

*W*hen the Mexicans shuck their dried corn for cooking, they throw a handful of ashes from the fire into water before adding the corn. This loosens the kernel's skin, thus making more of the corn's nutrients available. Crushed limestone works well in place of ashes. Several hours of simmering turns the corn soft and fluffy. The Mexicans call this *nixtamel.* To Americans, it is hulled corn or hominy.

In Colonial America, cornmeals and flours were made into dishes that are now classics in the South and in New England—hasty pudding, Indian pudding, succotash, and breads such as rye 'n' injun, Boston brown bread, corn bread, Johnnycake, and anadama bread. Young corn was roasted, boiled, or steamed; it went into pancakes or, best of all, corn chowder in a thousand variations.

The Italians make *polenta* of yellow cornmeal, and it often takes the place of bread in northern Italy. The Italians bolster the polenta with cheese, tomato sauce, cream, mushrooms, or any other tasty means of nutritional support.

Which is best to use—white cornmeal or yellow? White cornmeal, when cooked, has a slightly rougher texture than the yellow, but there is so little difference in flavor that the two are virtually interchangeable in recipes. Most cooks do use the color specified in a recipe primarily to get the intended texture. Shop for stone-ground cornmeal. It retains the nutritious, flavorful germ.

2 cups cornmeal mush

1 cup cooked bulgur

½ cup chopped peanuts

¼ cup sesame seeds

Cornmeal-Bulgur Patties

Preheat oven to 350°F.

Combine all ingredients and form into patties about 2½ inches in diameter. Place on a lightly greased baking sheet and bake 30 to 40 minutes.

Note: For a cocktail snack that is tasty and different, make patties about 1 inch in diameter and ½ inch thick. Serve hot or cold. The recipe will make about 3 dozen small patties.

Makes 1 dozen large patties

Cornbean Pie

Crust:

2 cups yellow cornmeal

2 tablespoons nutritional yeast

3 tablespoons oil

½ cup hot stock, or enough to make stiff batter

Filling:

1 medium-size onion, chopped

½ cup chopped carrots

½ cup chopped celery

1 clove garlic, minced

½ cup chopped green peppers

2 tablespoons oil

1 cup kidney beans, cooked

pinch of cayenne

1 tablespoon cumin

½ cup chopped tomatoes

3 tablespoons tamari soy sauce

⅓ cup grated sharp cheese

*P*reheat oven to 350°F.

Mix together all ingredients for crust and pat into a well-oiled 9-inch pie plate.

Saute onion, carrots, celery, garlic, and green peppers in oil about 5 minutes.

Add beans and spices and put into cornmeal crust.

Combine tomatoes with tamari and pour over the beans. Bake about 25 minutes. Remove from oven, sprinkle with cheese, and bake 5 minutes longer.

Serves 6

1½ cups milk

3 tablespoons butter

⅓ cup yellow cornmeal

1 cup shredded sharp Cheddar
   cheese

5 egg yolks

2 tablespoons chopped green
   onions

5 egg whites

Cornmeal Puff

*P*reheat oven to 350°F.

In the top of a double boiler, cook the milk, butter, and cornmeal, stirring occasionally, until thick and steaming (about 7 minutes). Remove from heat; stir in cheese, egg yolks, and green onions. Beat egg whites until stiff. Gently fold into cornmeal mixture.

Turn into a well-greased 2-quart ovenproof casserole. Place dish in a pan of hot water and bake 35 minutes.

Serves 6 to 8

Polenta Cheese Squares

5 cups cold water

1½ cups yellow cornmeal

1 cup grated sharp Cheddar cheese

⅓ cup grated Parmesan cheese

1½ cups tomato sauce

*I*n a large, heavy saucepan, bring water to a boil. Add cornmeal very slowly, stirring constantly with a wire whisk or long wooden spoon until mixture is thick and free of lumps.

Transfer cornmeal mixture to top of a double boiler. Place over boiling water and cook, covered, 30 minutes, stirring occasionally. Cornmeal is finished when it leaves sides of pan.

Remove from heat and turn cornmeal mixture into a lightly oiled 9 × 9 × 2-inch baking pan; cool and refrigerate until stiff enough to cut (3 to 4 hours or overnight).

Preheat oven to 400°F. Cut polenta into 16 squares. Arrange in an oiled baking dish. Sprinkle with Cheddar and Parmesan cheese and bake 15 minutes, or until cheese is melted and nicely browned. Serve immediately, topped with tomato sauce.

Serves 6 to 8

Note: Polenta may also be prepared by adding Cheddar cheese to cornmeal mixture just before removing from heat. Proceed as above. Sprinkle with Parmesan cheese before placing in oven.

1 cup yellow cornmeal

1 cup whole wheat flour

½ cup nonfat dry milk

2 teaspoons baking powder

2 eggs, beaten

1 cup buttermilk

3 tablespoons oil

Corn Bread

*P*reheat oven to 350°F.

Combine cornmeal, flour, dry milk, and baking powder. Make a well in the flour and add the remaining ingredients. Mix only until combined or wet.

Pour into a well-oiled 8-inch-square baking pan or dish. Bake 30 minutes, or until browned. Bread is done when a toothpick inserted in center comes out clean.

Makes 16 squares

Indian Pudding

4 cups milk

¼ cup butter

⅔ cup molasses

3 tablespoons honey

⅔ cup cornmeal

¾ teaspoon cinnamon

¾ teaspoon nutmeg

*H*eat 3 cups of milk. Stir in butter, molasses, and honey. Combine cornmeal and spices and stir gradually into warm milk mixture, using a wire whisk to avoid lumps. Cook over low heat, stirring constantly, about 10 minutes, or until thick.

Preheat oven to 300°F. Turn into an oiled ovenproof casserole, pour 1 cup milk over pudding (do not stir), and bake 3 hours.

Serves 6 to 8

MILLET

*T*he birds of North America eat a lot more millet than the humans in North America do. It is among the least familiar of the grains in this country. Still, millet is a common food to more people of the world than are wheat, rye, rice, or any other grain. The ancient Romans ate millet-grain paste and the early Chinese made thin pancakes out of millet meal. In Africa, where millet is a common staple, it is known as the food of the poor, probably because it sustains them so well!

When used as a cereal, millet is cooked much the way rice is, then topped with fruit or maple syrup. Millet can be cooked in milk as a way to enhance the protein content of the grain and make that protein totally assimilable. Millet is appropriate whenever any other grain might be used, as a stuffing, a thickener, in a stew, or in place of potatoes. Millet can also be prepared like a rice pudding or baked into a dessert souffle—simple, but unusual and elegant.

Interesting millet dishes, incorporating cheeses, beans, and vegetables of all kinds, used as entrees, seem to be relatively modern creations. Millet main-course souffles, pilafs, and steamed puddings are popular among lovers of natural foods who want to enjoy the widest array of grains.

Whole Millet Crackers

5 tablespoons oil

1 tablespoon honey

½ cup water

¼ cup millet

½ cup millet flour

1 cup whole wheat flour

*P*reheat oven to 350°F.

Combine oil, honey, and water. Stir in millet, millet flour, and whole wheat flour. It may be necessary to knead dough to work in the last of the flour.

Roll out dough ⅛ inch thick on *buttered* baking sheet. Do not use oil, as crackers may be difficult to loosen. Score crackers with a knife in square or diamond shapes and bake 20 minutes, or until golden brown. Remove from baking sheet and cool on a rack.

Makes 4 dozen crackers

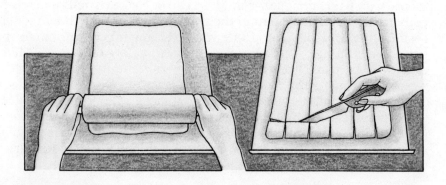

2 cups water

½ cup millet meal (whole millet
that has been ground in
a blender)

3 tablespoons oil

1 medium-size onion, chopped

1 cup raw cashews, ground

3 eggs, slightly beaten

⅔ cup wheat germ

½ cup skim milk powder

¼ cup chopped parsley

¼ cup chopped pimiento

½ cup water

⅛ teaspoon each of the following
herbs: ground sage,
rosemary, and marjoram

⅛ teaspoon mace

Cashew-
Millet
Casserole

*P*reheat oven to 325°F.

In top of a double boiler, bring 2 cups of water to a boil; add millet meal to rapidly boiling water very slowly, stirring constantly with a wire whisk to avoid lumping. Place over hot water and continue to cook 15 to 20 minutes, or until millet has absorbed all water. Remove from heat and cool slightly.

Heat oil in a skillet and saute onion.

Combine cooked millet and cashews in a mixing bowl. Add eggs, wheat germ, skim milk powder, sauteed onion, parsley, and pimiento. Add ½ cup water, blending together thoroughly. Stir in herbs, then mace. Adjust seasoning according to taste.

Turn mixture into an oiled 1½-quart ovenproof casserole and bake, uncovered, 45 minutes, or until tested to firmness and lightly browned. Serve immediately.

Serves 6 to 8

Creative Casserole

2 cups water

½ cup lentils

½ cup millet

3 medium-size or small broccoli stems, sliced

4 carrots, sliced

2 stalks celery, sliced

1 small onion, sliced

½ pound green beans, sliced in half lengthwise

oil as needed

tamari soy sauce to taste (about ⅓ cup)

¼ cup chopped parsley

Sauce:

2 stalks celery, sliced

4 medium-size parsnips, sliced

½ cup chopped parsley

*B*ring water to a boil, add lentils and millet and simmer 15 minutes, or until all the water has been absorbed. Set aside.

In a cast-iron skillet or wok, saute the broccoli stems, carrots, celery, onion, and green beans in oil and tamari until the vegetables just begin to soften. Add parsley. Set aside.

Saute celery and parsnips in a small amount of oil until tender. Put sauteed vegetables and parsley in a blender with a small amount of water. Puree and then heat through.

Combine lentil and millet mixture with the sauteed vegetables and top with sauce and additional parsley, if desired.

Serves 6

1 medium-size onion, finely
chopped

1 pound ground beef

1 tablespoon oil

2 cups water or stock

2 cups mushrooms

1 cup millet

6 cups water

2 tablespoons arrowroot

Meatballs, Millet, and Mushroom Gravy

*M*ix half the onion with meat and form into 1-inch meatballs.

Brown in oil, then add 2 cups water or stock, remaining onion, and mushrooms. Simmer 30 minutes.

Cook millet in 5 cups of boiling water 20 minutes over medium-high heat. Turn off heat, cover, and let stand until all the water is absorbed.

For the gravy, mix 1 cup cold water with arrowroot. Stir until all is dissolved in the water. Then pour at once into the meatballs and mushrooms in the pan, stirring until it thickens. Serve the meatballs and mushroom gravy over the millet.

Serves 5 to 6

Millet-
Lentil Loaf

½ cup millet

1 cup lentils

2 green onions, thinly sliced

¼ cup oil

2 cups coarsely chopped spinach

2 eggs, beaten

2 apples, grated

1 tablespoon ground coriander

1 tablespoon lemon juice

Cook millet according to preferred method (see Index). Cook lentils and drain if necessary.

Preheat oven to 350°F. Saute green onions in oil for a minute, then add spinach and toss lightly to steam for another minute or two. Combine cooked millet, lentils, sauteed vegetables, and remaining ingredients. Turn into an oiled loaf pan and bake 30 to 40 minutes, or until firm and golden brown on top. Serve warm.

Serves 4 to 6

4 cups water

2 tablespoons oil

1 cup millet meal (whole millet
that has been ground in
blender)

4 egg yolks

¼ cup skim milk powder

1 cup water

½ teaspoon crushed dill seeds
(optional)

3 tablespoons minced chives or
grated onions

1 cup grated or shredded sharp
cheese

4 egg whites

Millet
Souffle

*P*reheat oven to 350°F.

In a saucepan, bring 4 cups water to a boil. Add oil. Gradually add millet meal to boiling water, stirring constantly with a wire whisk until all of it has been incorporated. Place in top of a double boiler and cook about 20 to 30 minutes, or until all water has been absorbed. Stir mixture occasionally. Remove from heat and cool slightly.

In a large mixing bowl, beat egg yolks until thick. Combine skim milk powder with 1 cup water, using a wire whisk, and beat gradually into yolk mixture.

With beater set at medium speed, blend cooked millet into yolk mixture until thoroughly combined. Stir in dill seeds, if desired, and chives or onions. Add cheese.

Beat egg whites until soft peaks form; gently fold into millet mixture.

Pour mixture into a 2-quart ovenproof casserole and bake 35 to 45 minutes. Remove from oven and serve immediately.

Serves 6

Millet-Stuffed Peppers

½ cup millet

4 green peppers, halved, cored, and seeded

1 medium-size onion, minced

½ pound ground beef

1 tablespoon oil

2 tablespoons chopped parsley

1 teaspoon dried oregano

2 tablespoons wheat germ

1 tablespoon Parmesan cheese

1 cup tomato sauce

Cook millet according to preferred method (see Index).

Steam peppers 5 minutes. Saute onion and beef in oil about 5 minutes, stirring to brown meat evenly.

Preheat oven to 350°F. Combine millet with meat mixture, add herbs, and stuff into pepper halves. Top with wheat germ and Parmesan cheese and bake 20 minutes. Serve with tomato sauce.

Serves 4 to 6

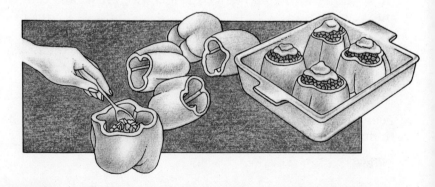

OATS

*I*n the nineteenth century, Scottish universities traditionally observed Oatmeal Monday—the day when poor students' parents would arrive with a sack of oatmeal to insure their sons' nourishment through the coming winter term. And few foods could have done more to help a young man through those brutal Scottish winters.

In Switzerland, this hearty, tasty grain is the base for *muësli,* a universal favorite that has nearly replaced fondue in the hearts of the Swiss. This mixture of fresh fruits, nuts, and oats was created in the nineteenth century by Dr. R. Bircher-Benner, as a healthful alternative to the rich and starchy foods favored by the Swiss at the turn of the century.

In buying oats to make oatmeal granola, cookies, or pastries, remember that "steel-cut" oats are the coarsest and most nutritious type. Old-fashioned "rolled" oats (oats milled into dry flakes by steel rollers) are good too, but finer and somewhat less nutritious. Steel-cut or rolled oats, simmered for 40 minutes in boiling water, then served with milk, cinnamon, fruit, or maple syrup, used to make the traditional American winter breakfast dish.

Cinnamon Oatmeal
with Raisins and Seeds

2 cups water

½ cup raisins

1 cup rolled oats

½ teaspoon vanilla

1 teaspoon cinnamon

¼ cup sunflower or sesame seeds

In a 1-quart saucepan, combine water and raisins. Bring to a boil.

Add oats gradually and stir. Add vanilla and cinnamon. Cook 10 minutes. Pour into bowls and top with seeds. Serve with milk or yogurt.

Serves 4

Natural Quick-Cooking Oats

The instant oatmeal breakfast sold in supermarkets is not the most desirable way to save time in the morning. These commercial products usually have additives and artificial flavorings and, in the case of the breakfast envelopes, lots of salt. If you really do not have the time to cook your breakfast oatmeal for a few more minutes, soak the oats the evening before and just bring it to a boil the next morning. This way you will have homemade instant oatmeal, cheap and additive-free.

3 cups rolled oats

1 cup wheat or rye flakes

½ cup wheat germ

½ cup bran

½ cup sesame seeds

½ cup cashews or walnuts

½ cup sunflower seeds

½ cup shredded coconut

¼ cup oil

¼ cup honey

1 cup raisins

Granola

*P*reheat oven to 225°F.

Combine all ingredients in a large bowl and spread in a thin layer on a baking sheet and bake about 1 hour. It should turn a golden brown.

When the granola is browned, add raisins.

Yields 8 cups

Oatmeal Soup

½ cup oatmeal

½ small onion, finely chopped

1 large clove garlic, minced

1 tablespoon oil or melted butter

¾ cup chopped tomatoes

4 cups any soup stock

2 tablespoons soy grits

2 teaspoons tamari soy sauce

*I*n an iron skillet or heavy-bottom saucepan, toast oatmeal over medium-high heat, stirring constantly to keep it from burning, until it is light brown. Remove oatmeal from pan and set aside.

Saute onion and garlic in oil or butter until tender. Combine with tomatoes, soup stock, soy grits, and toasted oatmeal and cook over low heat about 5 minutes. Season with tamari and serve.

Yields about 4 cups

1 cup brown rice

⅓ cup chopped green peppers

⅓ cup chopped onions

⅓ cup chopped celery

1 egg, beaten

⅓ cup cornmeal

⅓ cup rolled oats

⅓ cup wheat germ

1 tablespoon tamari soy sauce

2 tablespoons rye flour

2 tablespoons wheat germ

2 tablespoons oil

Grainburgers

Cook rice according to preferred method (see Index).

Combine cooked rice, vegetables, egg, and grains. Mold into patties. Dust with mixture of 2 tablespoons flour and 2 tablespoons wheat germ. Add tamari. In a hot skillet, brown in oil on both sides.

Makes 6 to 8 patties

Note: As an extra touch, add a slice of cheese after you have turned the patty to brown on the second side.

2 pounds lean ground beef
(chuck or round)

⅓ cup wheat germ

½ cup oatmeal

2 tablespoons chopped parsley

½ teaspoon freshly ground pepper

½ cup chopped onions

2 tablespoons oil

2 eggs

¼ cup skim milk powder

½ cup water

½ cup tomato juice

Molded Meat Loaf with Oatmeal

*P*reheat oven to 350°F.

In a large mixing bowl, combine ground beef, wheat germ, oatmeal, parsley, and pepper; set aside.

Saute onions in oil until tender but not brown; add to meat mixture.

Beat eggs lightly. Combine skim milk powder and water with a wire whisk and add to eggs. Blend together and add to meat mixture; then add tomato juice. Mix thoroughly.

Oil a 9 × 5 × 3-inch loaf pan. Turn meat mixture into pan, packing down well. Allow to rest 10 to 15 minutes in refrigerator.

Run spatula around edge of meat loaf to loosen. Carefully turn out into a lightly oiled shallow baking pan, keeping original shape as much as possible. Brush surface with oil.

Place meat loaf on middle rack of oven and bake 1 hour and 15 minutes. Remove from oven when nicely browned and allow to rest 10 minutes before serving.

Serves 6 to 8

2 tablespoons dry yeast

6 tablespoons lukewarm water

6 teaspoons honey

2 cups oatmeal, ground to a
    coarse flour in an electric
    blender

2 tablespoons lukewarm milk or
    light cream

2 eggs, beaten

2 tablespoons melted butter

Scottish Scones or Bannocks

*D*issolve yeast in lukewarm water to which 2 teaspoons honey have been added. Add yeast mixture to oat flour along with milk or cream and 4 teaspoons honey. Mix well, cover, and set aside in a warm place 1 hour. Combine beaten eggs and melted butter and stir into batter. Cover again and set aside for 1 more hour.

Preheat oven to 400°F. For scones, drop by the tablespoonful into an oiled iron skillet and bake 10 minutes. For bannocks, pour batter all at once into a large oiled skillet (about 10-inch) and bake as for scones. Cut into wedges before serving. Serve hot with butter and honey.

Serves 6 (about 2 dozen scones or 1 large bannock)

Oatmeal-Walnut Cake

1½ cups boiling water

1 cup rolled oats

½ cup butter

¾ cup honey

2 eggs

1¼ cups whole wheat flour

2 tablespoons coarse bran

2 tablespoons lecithin granules

2 tablespoons wheat germ

2 teaspoons bone meal powder

1 teaspoon baking powder

1 teaspoon baking soda

1 teaspoon cinnamon

½ cup chopped walnuts

*P*reheat oven to 350°F.

Pour boiling water over oats and let it cool. Cream butter and honey, add eggs, then the slightly cooled oatmeal. In another bowl, combine the flour with the rest of the ingredients and blend this thoroughly with the oatmeal mixture. Bake in a greased and floured 9-inch-square baking pan 40 minutes.

This cake is delicious just as it is, but if you want to fancy it up, try this topping.

6 tablespoons butter

¼ cup light cream

¼ cup honey

1 cup shredded coconut

½ cup chopped nuts

1 teaspoon vanilla

Topping for Oatmeal-Walnut Cake

*M*ix all ingredients together then spread on cooled cake. Brown under broiler briefly.

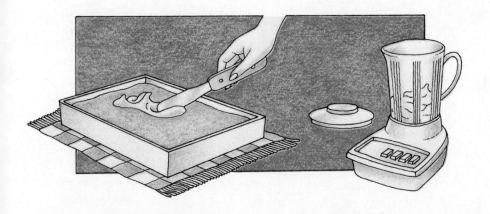

Oatmeal Macaroons

2 egg whites

⅓ cup maple syrup

1 cup rolled oats

½ cup grated coconut

Preheat oven to 350°F.

Beat egg whites in a small bowl until stiff.

Combine maple syrup and oats in another bowl and mix until well blended. Add coconut. Fold in beaten whites.

Drop by the teaspoonful onto parchment-lined baking sheet. Bake 12 minutes.

Makes 20 to 24 macaroons

¾ cup soy flour

½ cup skim milk powder

½ cup raisins or chopped dates

½ cup chopped walnuts

1½ cups wheat germ

2 cups rolled oats

½ cup oil

½ cup honey

2 tablespoons blackstrap
molasses

2 eggs

2 teaspoons vanilla

Oatmeal-Wheat Germ Cookies

Preheat oven to 350°F.

Sift soy flour and milk powder together. Add raisins or dates, walnuts, wheat germ, and rolled oats.

In another bowl, combine oil, honey, and molasses. Add eggs, one at a time, beating after each. Stir in vanilla.

Combine dry and wet ingredients. Blend well.

Drop by the teaspoonful onto buttered baking sheets or sheets covered with foil. Bake 10 minutes.

Makes about 6 dozen cookies

RICE

Of the 7,000 varieties of rice in the world, comprising a multitude of colors, textures, flavors, and aromas, Americans eat 2. White long-grain rice accounts for 99 percent of our rice diet, and brown rice accounts for the other 1 percent. We are definitely missing something.

In the cultures that consume large quantities of rice, the subtleties of its preparation and consumption provide true pleasure and are of great significance. East Indians, for example, enjoy rice with an enthusiasm, originality, and religious reverence we can hardly imagine. It might be served there as a plain accompaniment or as a main dish; it might be boiled, steamed, or baked in water or broth; it might be adorned with spices, tinted yellow with turmeric or saffron, or ground fine to make a smooth dessert.

If you are undecided about which type of rice to use—brown or white—consider that brown rice is coated with bran, which holds many valuable nutrients and gives it a rich, nutty, more definite taste than white rice has. To make white rice, twentieth-century milling machines efficiently strip the bran layer from the rice kernel, leaving a pure white, all-carbohydrate grain, virtually barren of vitamins and minerals. Like white bread, white rice is "enriched"—an attempt to put back some of the nutrition removed with the bran. Two B vitamins, thiamine and niacin, are sprayed on, along with iron. But other nutrients that exist in the discarded bran layer are lost forever.

1½ cups brown rice

2 tablespoons butter

2 tablespoons whole wheat
flour

2¼ cups beef stock

1 teaspoon chopped chives

½ teaspoon dried thyme

2 teaspoons curry powder

4 eggs

2 tablespoons chopped parsley

Eggs on Curried Rice

Cook rice according to preferred method (see Index). Preheat oven to 350°F.

Pack cooked rice firmly into a buttered baking dish. Make four little wells, evenly spaced, about 1 inch deep, on the surface of the rice. Melt butter in a saucepan, add flour, stirring, and then add beef stock, stirring constantly. Cook until thickened. Add herbs and curry powder.

Spoon approximately 1 cup of the sauce over the rice into the wells. Break an egg into each well, gently spoon the remaining sauce over the entire surface, and bake 25 minutes, or until eggs are firm. Garnish with parsley and serve.

Serves 4

1 teaspoon kelp powder

1 teaspoon paprika

1 3- or 4-pound chicken, cut into 8 pieces

4 tablespoons oil

Chicken with Cherries and Brown Rice

2 large onions, sliced

½ cup chicken stock

2 cups pitted bing cherries, fresh or frozen

2 tablespoons honey

2 tablespoons water or fruit juice

1½ cups long-grain brown rice

4 cups water

¼ cup oil

Combine kelp and paprika and sprinkle over chicken pieces. Heat 4 tablespoons of oil in a large skillet and add the chicken pieces a few at a time. Cook about 5 minutes on each side to brown.

Remove chicken and brown onions in the skillet just ever so lightly. Put chicken pieces back in the skillet, add chicken stock, and bring to a boil. Then reduce heat to low, cover the pan, and simmer 30 minutes, or until fork tender.

While the chicken is simmering, put the cherries, honey, and 2 tablespoons water or juice in a saucepan over very low heat. Simmer, uncovered, 3 minutes, stirring frequently. Remove from heat.

Chicken with Cherries and Brown Rice — continued

Partially cook rice in a large saucepan. Bring 4 cups of water to a boil, add rice, and simmer 20 minutes. Drain rice through a strainer.

Transfer chicken pieces to a plate, reserving 2 tablespoons of the cooking liquid and the browned onions.

Combine reserved cooking liquid and the ¼ cup oil in a large pot or ovenproof casserole and mix well. Put half the rice in the casserole, spreading it out evenly. Add chicken pieces, onions, and half the cherries. Arrange the rest of the rice on top of the mixture. Put in the remaining cherries with their cooking liquid, cover the casserole, and simmer 20 minutes, or until rice is tender.

To serve, arrange chicken pieces and onions on top of the bed of rice. Cover the chicken with the cherries.

Serves 4

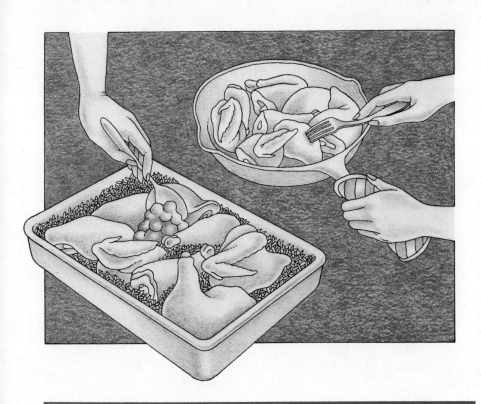

Kedgeree

1 cup brown rice

1 pound fish filet

3 tablespoons butter

2 hard-cooked eggs, chopped

pinch of pepper

Cook rice according to preferred method (see Index).

Simmer fish filet in a little water until fish flakes easily (about 5 to 10 minutes). Drain and set aside.

Melt butter in saucepan. Add cooked rice, fish, eggs, and pepper. Stir gently over moderate heat until hot.

Serves 4

Have You Tried These Rice Products?

Consider adding these nutritious and tasty rice products available in most natural foods stores to your pantry stock:

Rice polishings, the inner layer of bran that is left over in the production of white rice, can be added to soups, sauces, and the batter of baked goods.

Rice bran, the outer bran layer that is a by-product yielded by the processing of brown rice, can be also used in baked goods.

Rice grits, coarsely cracked brown rice, can be added to soups, stews, and casseroles.

Brown rice flour, made from ground short-grain brown rice, can be added to other flours for baking.

Short-grain brown rice, starchier and stickier when cooked than long-grain, is used primarily in Japanese cooking.

Long-grain brown rice, used in Chinese, Indian, Indonesian, and Middle-Eastern cooking, is dry and fluffy when cooked.

Sweet brown rice, a short-grain brown rice with high sugar and starch content, is suited to Oriental rice cakes and puddings.

2 tablespoons oil

1 pound lean chopped beef

2 large onions, chopped

1 large green pepper, chopped

3 stalks celery, chopped

1 clove garlic, minced

½ cup brown rice

1 cup water

2 cups chopped tomatoes

pepper to taste

Spanish Brown Rice and Meat

*H*eat oil in a large saucepan and brown meat and vegetables. Add rice and water and simmer 30 minutes. Add tomatoes and pepper and continue cooking about 30 minutes, or until rice is tender, adding more liquid if necessary.

Serves 4 to 6

Brown Rice, as Easy as White

Brown rice requires only minutes more cooking time, yet adds so much more to meals than the blander-tasting white. It is an excellent change from potatoes and can be used as the base for an infinite variety of appetizing dishes, including pilafs, salads, casseroles, and baked goods.

Spinach and Rice Casserole

2 cups cooked brown rice

1 cup grated Cheddar cheese

4 eggs, beaten

4 tablespoons chopped parsley

1 pound spinach, chopped

4 tablespoons wheat germ

1 tablespoon oil

Preheat oven to 350°F.

Combine rice and cheese. Add eggs and parsley.

Stir in spinach and pour into an oiled ovenproof casserole. Top with wheat germ that has been mixed with the oil and bake 35 minutes.

Serves 6 to 8

¼ cup finely chopped onions

¼ cup finely chopped green
peppers

¼ cup finely chopped celery

2 to 3 tablespoons oil

3 cups cooked long-grain brown
rice, cooked 1 day ahead

½ cup cooked green peas

½ cup diced cooked chicken

3 eggs, slightly beaten

¼ cup bean sprouts

tamari soy sauce (optional)

Fried Rice

Saute onions, green peppers, and celery in 2 tablespoons oil in a skillet until just tender. Remove from pan.

Add more oil to pan, if necessary, and saute rice. Add sauteed vegetables, peas, chicken, and eggs.

Stir 2 or 3 minutes, or until eggs are set but not dry or brown. Add bean sprouts. Season with tamari to taste, if desired. Serve at once.

Serves 6 to 8

Pungent Rice

1 medium-size onion, finely chopped

3 tablespoons oil

1 cup brown rice

3 cups chicken stock

1 tablespoon chopped basil or ½ teaspoon dried

1 tablespoon chopped marjoram or 1 teaspoon dried

2 teaspoons chopped thyme or ¼ teaspoon dried

¼ teaspoon curry powder

chopped parsley for garnish

*I*n a medium-size saucepan or skillet, saute onion in oil. Add rice and continue to saute 5 minutes longer.

Add chicken stock, stirring constantly. Stir in remaining ingredients (except parsley). Heat to boiling. Lower heat, cover, and cook slowly 25 to 30 minutes without stirring, or until rice is tender and liquid is absorbed. Garnish with parsley.

Serves 5 to 6

1 cup brown rice

6 tablespoons olive oil

3 tablespoons cider vinegar

½ teaspoon dried tarragon

¼ cup chopped green peppers
   or pimientos

¼ cup chopped parsley

¼ cup finely chopped onions

½ cup cooked green peas

¼ cup chopped chives (optional)

Rice Salad

Cook rice according to preferred method (see Index). While still hot, add oil, vinegar, and tarragon. Cool. Add remaining vegetables and mix well. Chill.

At serving time, pile rice salad on platter in the shape of a pyramid. Surround with wedges of tomato and hard-cooked eggs.

Serves 4

Rice Flour Muffins

2 cups brown rice flour

3 egg yolks, slightly beaten

2 tablespoons maple syrup or honey

1 cup milk

2 tablespoons oil

3 egg whites, stiffly beaten

Preheat oven to 400°F.

Combine all ingredients except egg whites. Mix thoroughly and beat with a whisk until light (about 2 minutes). Fold in egg whites. Pour into oiled muffin tins and bake 20 minutes, or until done.

Makes 1 dozen muffins

¼ cup sesame seeds

 2 tablespoons skim milk powder

¼ cup water

2 egg yolks

2 tablespoons whole wheat flour

⅛ teaspoon pepper

⅔ cup cooked brown rice

 2 egg whites, stiffly beaten

 oil for frying

Sesame-Rice Fritters

*T*oast sesame seeds until golden (about 20 minutes in a 200°F oven).

Mix skim milk powder and water with a wire whisk. Add egg yolks, flour, and pepper.

Combine milk mixture, sesame seeds, and rice; mix well. Fold in egg whites.

Drop by the tablespoonful onto hot, oiled griddle and fry until brown. Drain on paper towel.

Makes 16 fritters

Old-Fashioned Rice Pudding

½ cup brown rice

1 cup skim milk powder

3½ cups water

⅓ cup honey

¼ teaspoon ground or grated nutmeg

⅓ cup raisins

Wash rice and remove any foreign particles.

In top of a double boiler, combine skim milk powder, water, honey, rice, and nutmeg.

Cook, covered, over hot water 2½ hours, or until rice is tender. Stir mixture occasionally.

During the last 30 minutes of cooking, stir in raisins. Serve warm or cold.

Serves 5 to 6

RYE

*R*ye, once a mere weed in wheatfields, long ago proved its ability to nourish and its versatility as a grain for baking. This persistent "weed" was used by medieval cooks in a mixture with pea and barley flours to make the daily brown bread.

No food better exploits the full rich pungency of the rye grain's flavor than German pumpernickel bread. Made with unrefined rye flour and molasses, it is much blacker and heavier than the rye bread Americans usually eat. Russians and Scandinavians also give the rye grain its due. Russians seldom sit down to a meal without great slices of dark rye bread, accompanied by sweet butter or cheese. Rye crisp bread, or *knacke*, in Scandinavia is baked from unsifted whole rye flour. For uses other than bread, the dark brown rye grains may be boiled like rice for a hearty cereal or added to other grains for dishes with a chewier texture.

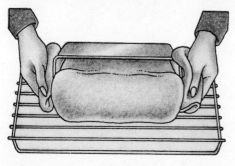

2½ cups water

1 cup rye, toasted in dry skillet
   and "cracked" in electric
   blender

Hot Rye and Peanut Cereal

½ cup peanut flour

¼ cup raisins

1 tablespoon honey

1 tablespoon molasses

2 tablespoons wheat germ

2 tablespoons sesame seeds

Bring water to a boil in a 2-quart saucepan. Stir rye into boiling water. Add peanut flour and raisins and cook 10 to 15 minutes, or until rye is tender. Add honey, molasses, wheat germ, and sesame seeds. Serve warm with milk.

Serves 4

Note: Peanut flour may be bought at natural foods stores, or raw peanuts may be pulverized, ½ cup at a time, in an electric blender.

¾ cup rye berries

¾ cup barley

1½ cups water

2 onions, chopped

1 clove garlic, minced

4 tablespoons butter

2 tomatoes, chopped

4 eggs, beaten

½ teaspoon dried basil

½ teaspoon chopped sage

1 teaspoon chopped parsley

3 stalks celery, chopped

1 green pepper, chopped

2 tablespoons melted butter

chopped Brazil and hazel
    nuts (optional)

Rye and Barley Loaf

Soak rye and barley overnight. Simmer grains in water 1½ hours, or until tender. Add more water as necessary.

Preheat oven to 350°F. In a large skillet, saute onions and garlic in 4 tablespoons of butter until tender. Add tomatoes and cook until mixture resembles puree. Add grains, eggs, herbs, celery, and green pepper. Pour into a greased 9 × 5-inch loaf pan, brush with 2 tablespoons of melted butter, and bake 50 minutes. Turn out of pan, slice, and garnish with chopped nuts, if desired.

Serves 12

½ cup rye

½ cup lentils

1 small onion, minced

½ cup diced carrots

½ cup diced celery

1 tablespoon oil

1 teaspoon caraway seeds
(optional)

¼ teaspoon dried thyme

¼ teaspoon dried sage

3 cups chicken stock

Rye and
Lentil Pilaf

Cook rye according to preferred method (see Index). Cook lentils. Drain rye and lentils, reserving liquids for soup.

Saute onion, carrots, and celery in oil until tender. Combine with cooked rye and lentils. Add herbs and chicken stock, cover, and steam 10 minutes, or until hot.

Serves 4

¾ cup water

¾ cup nonfat dry milk

¾ cup rye or whole wheat flour

Sourdough Starter

Using a glass or stainless steel bowl, reconstitute milk by combining water and nonfat dry milk. Cover loosely with a cloth and leave at room temperature 2 or 3 days until it smells sour. It is not necessary to leave it until it is thick or clabbered.

When the milk smells sour, stir in rye or whole wheat flour. Leave again at room temperature 3 or 4 days, until there seems to be some "action" in it. Look for small holes, evidence of gas forming and being given off.

When the starter seems to be "working," it should be "doubled" by adding 1 cup reconstituted milk (as above) and ¾ cup rye or whole wheat flour, just as you did the first time.

Leave this "doubled" starter at room temperature a few hours and then refrigerate it in a glass or plastic container, large enough so there is no danger of it overflowing. It can also be frozen.

How Starters Started

As with many other startling discoveries, the use of sourdough starter followed from a chance meeting of elements. The first leaven is believed to have been discovered and used in ancient Egypt after some favorable microorganisms drifted into a fresh piece of dough that had been left while the baker went off for a few hours. Up to that time, all breads were flat. The bread baked from this slightly risen dough was lighter and more appetizing than the usual product. The fermentation process responsible for this was soon guessed at and repeated.

½ cup cornmeal

1 cup cracked wheat

2 cups cracked rye (rye can be "cracked" in an electric blender)

3½ cups boiling water

1 cup sourdough starter

½ cup lukewarm water

½ cup molasses

2 teaspoons dry yeast

2¾ cups rye flour

3 cups whole wheat flour

Sourdough Pumpernickel Bread

Combine cornmeal, cracked wheat, and cracked rye and pour boiling water over them, stirring briskly to avoid lumping. Cool to lukewarm and add sourdough starter, stirring it in until dough is smooth. This is the "sponge." Leave overnight in a warm place (a turned-off oven is a good spot). Next day remove 1 cup of sponge, combine it with 1 cup lukewarm water, and refrigerate for future use.

Combine ½ cup lukewarm water and 1 tablespoon of the molasses. Sprinkle dry yeast over surface and set aside 5 minutes, until yeast is softened. Add yeast mixture and remaining molasses to sponge; then add rye flour and whole wheat flour, reserving some for kneading. Knead dough until no longer sticky. Place dough in a large oiled bowl, first putting it upside down to coat surface with oil, and then placing it right side up. Cover with a cloth and set in turned-off oven 2½ hours to rise.

Punch dough down and form into 1 large loaf or 2 smaller loaves. Place each in an oiled ovenproof casserole. Cover again with towel and let rise 1 hour. Preheat oven to 200°F. Cover casserole tightly with foil and/or lid and bake 3 to 4 hours. Place a pan of water on the lowest shelf of the oven and leave it there throughout the baking process. When bread is done (inserted toothpick comes out clean), remove it from casserole and cool before slicing.

Makes 1 large loaf or 2 small loaves

4 teaspoons dry yeast

½ cup lukewarm water

⅓ cup honey

1 tablespoon grated orange rind

1 teaspoon anise seeds

1 teaspoon caraway seeds

⅓ cup molasses

2 tablespoons oil

1¼ cups hot water

4 cups rye flour

2½ cups whole wheat flour

1 egg, lightly beaten with ½ teaspoon water

Swedish Limpa Rye Bread

Sprinkle yeast over lukewarm water. Add 1 teaspoon honey and let stand 5 to 10 minutes.

Meanwhile, put remaining honey, orange rind, anise seed, caraway seed, molasses, and oil into a large bowl.

Pour hot water into this mixture and stir well. Cool to lukewarm. Blend in 1 cup rye flour, beating until smooth.

Stir softened yeast into mixture, beating well. Add remaining 3 cups rye flour, mixing until smooth. Beat in whole wheat flour with a spoon, turning dough out onto a board to knead in the rest of the flour if necessary. Let rest 10 minutes.

Knead dough until smooth and no longer sticky. Put it into an oiled bowl, cover with a damp cloth, and set it in a warm place until doubled in bulk (about 1 hour).

Punch dough down. Cover and let rise again until nearly doubled in bulk (about 1 hour).

Shape into 2 loaves and place either in 8 × 3½-inch oiled bread pans or on a baking sheet. Brush with beaten egg. Let rise 30 minutes or so more.

Preheat oven to 350°F and bake 45 to 50 minutes, or until a deep golden brown. Remove from pan and cool on a rack. Store in refrigerator.

Makes 2 loaves

Old Country Soft Pretzel Sticks

1 tablespoon dry yeast

1¼ cups lukewarm water

1 tablespoon honey

4½ cups rye flour

1 egg, beaten with ½ teaspoon water

1 medium-size onion, chopped, sauteed, and drained on paper towel

Soften yeast in lukewarm water. Add honey and set mixture aside 5 minutes. Then stir in 4 cups rye flour.

Turn dough onto lightly floured board and knead with ½ cup rye flour until smooth. Divide dough into 48 pieces and roll each into a rope about ½ inch in diameter and 5 inches long. Place on a buttered baking sheet.

Brush with egg and water glaze and sprinkle with onion. Let rise 20 to 30 minutes. Preheat oven to 425°F and bake 15 to 20 minutes. Cool on a rack.

Makes 48 sticks

Note: Caraway seeds, sesame seeds, or poppy seeds may be substituted for the onion.

Is the Dough Ready to Knead?

If you are in doubt, sprinkle a tablespoon of flour around the edges of the bowl and over the top of the dough. Then stir it up and over to coat the sides and bottom and "unstick" the dough from the bowl. With a wooden spoon, scoop up the dough in the bowl and lift it. If it holds together for a second or two before it drops back into the bowl, it is ready to knead.

2 egg yolks

¼ cup honey

2 tablespoons soft butter

1 cup apple juice

1½ cups soft rye bread crumbs
   or ¾ cup dry crumbs

¼ teaspoon cinnamon

1 cup fresh raspberries, blueberries, or other berries

2 egg whites, stiffly beaten

Rye Bread Berry Pudding

*P*reheat oven to 325°F.

Beat egg yolks and honey together. Add butter and beat in to blend. Add apple juice, bread crumbs, cinnamon, and berries. Carefully fold in egg whites.

Pour into an ungreased ovenproof casserole and bake 45 minutes, or until set. Cool slightly and serve pudding warm with cream or yogurt.

Serves 4

Tiny Cream Puffs

1 cup water

½ cup butter

1 cup rye or whole wheat flour

4 eggs

*P*reheat oven to 400°F.

Bring water and butter to a boil in a medium-size saucepan. Remove pan from heat. Add flour all at once, stirring hard with a wooden spoon. Lower heat and continue to cook dough, stirring constantly, for a minute or two to make sure flour is cooked. Transfer dough to bowl of an electric mixer.

Add eggs, one at a time, beating well after each addition.

Drop dough by the teaspoonful onto a lightly buttered baking sheet, leaving 1 inch between each puff. Bake 25 to 30 minutes, or until they are quite firm. Loosen carefully with a spatula and cool on a wire rack. Store in a cool dry place until time to split and fill them. Filling should be done just before serving to prevent them from getting soggy.

Makes about 6 dozen 1½-inch puffs

TRITICALE

*T*riticale, the youngest of all grains, is a crossbreed of wheat and rye. Its name derives from *triticum* and *secale,* the Latin words for wheat and rye. The new grain successfully combined the productivity of wheat with the ruggedness of rye. Triticale contains significantly more protein than most other cereal grains. It is a high-quality protein—rich in lysine and methionine, amino acids that are low in most grains. With this improved amino acid balance, triticale has a biological value close to that of eggs and meat. This new grain is available in many natural foods stores.

Triticale flour can be used in breads, cookies, and pancakes, either by itself or mixed with other flour. It gives a pleasing nutty flavor to bread. For a lighter loaf use a 50:50 ratio when mixing it with whole wheat flour.

The grains may be cooked and used in other baked goods and casseroles as rye and wheat grains are used.

Another way to use triticale is to sprout it. It sprouts quickly and easily and has a wonderful chewy texture. Add the sprouts to salads, casseroles, to brown rice dishes, to soups, or just snack on them. (Don't let sprouts get any longer than the grain itself. They will continue to grow in the refrigerator and must be used quickly.)

Triticale, Cheese, and Nut Casserole

1 tablespoon oil

1 tablespoon butter

1 medium-size onion, chopped

3 large stalks celery with leaves, chopped

½ cup chopped cashews

½ cup chopped walnuts

½ cup sunflower seeds

1 cup cooked triticale

1 cup ricotta cheese

2 teaspoons chopped chives

2 tablespoons chopped parsley

1 tablespoon chopped thyme or 1½ teaspoons dried

2 eggs, lightly beaten

¼ cup wheat germ

¼ cup sesame seeds

*P*reheat oven to 350°F.

In a large skillet, heat oil and butter and then saute onion until limp. Add celery, cover, and cook 5 minutes.

In a mixing bowl, combine nuts, sunflower seeds, triticale, cheese, chives, parsley, thyme, and eggs. Add onion and celery mixture and mix thoroughly.

Grease a 1½-quart ovenproof casserole. Sprinkle half the wheat germ on the bottom and sides, then turn the mixture into the dish and sprinkle the remaining wheat germ and sesame seeds on top. Bake 1 hour.

Serves 6 to 8

2 tablespoons honey

½ cup lukewarm water

2 tablespoons dry yeast

2 teaspoons vinegar

1 cup milk

2 tablespoons oil

3 eggs, beaten

2 cups triticale flour

4 cups whole wheat flour

Triticale Egg Bread

*D*issolve honey in lukewarm water. Sprinkle yeast over surface and set aside 5 minutes to activate. Add vinegar to milk and heat just to lukewarm temperature, stirring constantly, until the milk curdles. Remove from heat and pour into a large bowl. Add oil, eggs, and triticale flour to soured milk. Add yeast mixture, stirring in well; then add 3 cups whole wheat flour, reserving approximately 1 cup for kneading.

Turn dough out onto a well-floured board or counter and knead a full 5 minutes. Place dough in an oiled bowl, turning it to oil surface. Cover and put in a warm place to rise about 1 hour and 15 minutes, or until doubled in bulk. Punch down dough. Let rise again about 30 minutes.

Form into 1 large loaf and 1 small loaf, place in buttered bread pans, and let rise another 30 minutes, or until dough is slightly rounded over the top of the pan. Preheat oven to 350°F and bake 30 to 35 minutes, or until done. Remove loaves from pans and cool on racks.

Makes 1 large and 1 small loaf

Making Dough with Nonfat Dry Milk

If you use nonfat dry milk to make dough, it can be dissolved right in the yeast-water mixture. One-third cup nonfat dry milk and 1 cup water equals 1 cup milk.

Herbed Triticale Casserole Bread

4 teaspoons dry yeast

1 cup lukewarm water

1 tablespoon honey

2 tablespoons minced onions

2 tablespoons butter

2½ cups triticale flour

1 cup yogurt

2 teaspoons dried basil

1 teaspoon dried oregano

2 teaspoons dried dillweed

2 cups whole wheat flour

In bowl of an electric mixer, soften yeast in lukewarm water to which honey has been added. Saute onions in butter until tender. Set aside to cool. When yeast mixture is active, add 2 cups triticale flour to it, stirring to blend. Add yogurt and then the sauteed onions and herbs. Beat at medium speed 2 minutes, scraping sides of bowl once during this time. Beat in ½ cup triticale flour and whole wheat flour.

Cover bowl with a clean, dampened towel and set in a warm place to rise 1 hour, or until almost doubled in size. Punch down dough, turn into a well-oiled 2-quart ovenproof casserole, and let rise 30 minutes.

Preheat oven to 375°F and bake 50 minutes. Turn loaf out onto wire rack and cool.

Makes 1 loaf

½ cup oil

½ cup honey or molasses

½ cup peanut butter

1 egg

½ teaspoon vanilla

1½ cups triticale flour

peanuts

Peanutty Peanut Butter Cookies

*P*reheat oven to 375°F.

Combine oil, honey or molasses, peanut butter, and egg. Beat well. Add remaining ingredients. Shape into balls and use a fork to flatten on a greased or parchment-lined baking sheet. Top each with a peanut half. Bake 8 to 10 minutes.

Makes about 2 dozen cookies

Triticale Dessert

1 cup triticale sprouts

2 tablespoons honey or maple syrup

1 tablespoon shredded coconut

2 tablespoons raisins, chopped dates, avocados, or any fresh fruit

1 cup yogurt, lightly chilled

Combine all ingredients and serve.

Serves 2 to 4

2 eggs, beaten

½ cup oil

½ cup honey

½ teaspoon vanilla

2½ cups triticale flour

1 teaspoon cinnamon

¼ teaspoon crushed anise
seeds
½ cup chopped walnuts

Triticale- Nut Drops

*P*reheat oven to 375°F.

Combine eggs, oil, honey, and vanilla. Combine flour, spices, and nuts and add to liquid ingredients. Drop by the teaspoonful onto buttered baking sheet, press flat with the bottom of a glass that has been dipped in water, and top with a walnut piece, if desired. Bake 12 to 15 minutes, or until golden brown. Cool on a rack.

Makes 4 dozen cookies

WHEAT

When Americans say "flour," they usually mean wheat flour. It is equally true that to most Americans wheat flour is bleached white flour. It gives baked goods the familiar cottony white look, and it puffs breads and cakes to a super high. But, in exchange, many of the nutritional values and much of the flavor that makes wheat a life-sustaining favorite are all but lost. Why buy the neutered bleached white flour when whole wheat grain is readily available? And why limit the use of whole wheat flour to baked goods or as a thickener for sauces when you can enjoy it in the variety of ways other cultures use it throughout the world?

The people of the Middle East turn wheat into bulgur by boiling whole wheat grains and leaving them to parch in the sun, then crushing them with a mortar and pestle. In *tabouli*, a fine grind of bulgur is briefly soaked, then mixed, uncooked, with fresh herbs (usually parsley and mint) and chopped green onions, and seasoned with olive oil and lemon juice.

Kibbi, using a slightly coarser grind of bulgur, is a spicy mixture of ground lamb and minced onion, served raw or cooked. Both the lamb and the bulgur are ground with a mortar and pestle in the arduous ancient method, ending up with a soft mixture that is patted into a flat, round cake. Lebanon considers kibbi its national dish, but Syria, Jordan, and Iraq all serve this familiar mixture meant to be eaten scooped up with bits of traditional flatbreads.

Other bulgur dishes include those made from bulgur steamed with broth, then fashioned into any of several types of pilaf and often made with onions.

Tracing the origins of these bulgur dishes is virtually impossible. People have always eaten them and played endless variations on them by adding and subtracting herbs, onions, and other condiments. They are subtle treatments of wheat by a people who have such a reverence for that grain that when a piece of bread is dropped on the floor in a Middle-Eastern home, it is immediately picked up and kissed.

In America, the various grades of bulgur are made by machine. Because it is precooked and then dried, bulgur stores well. Better yet, it is only minimally processed, so it retains most of the considerable nutrients whole wheat offers—rich protein, iron, riboflavin, niacin, and thiamine.

Like other grains, bulgur lends itself to the most basic cooking techniques. Cooked in twice its volume of water, as rice is, bulgur serves beautifully as a substitute for beans, chick-peas, potatoes, rice, or other foods.

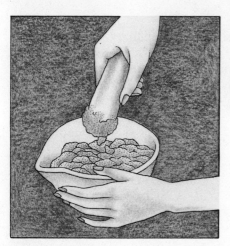 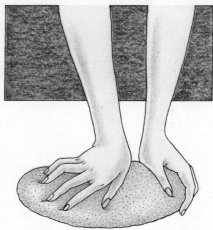

1¾ cups water

⅓ cup coarsely ground whole
  wheat cereal

1 teaspoon butter

1 cup cubed fresh fruit (apple,
  banana, and the like)

¼ cup raisins

honey to taste

milk to taste

Hot Wheat Cereal

*B*ring water to a boil. Slowly stir in wheat cereal. Cover, reduce heat, and simmer 15 minutes, stirring occasionally. Add butter, fruit, raisins, honey, and milk. Serve immediately.

Serves 2

¼ cup wheat berries

1 cup water

¼ cup oatmeal

1 cup yogurt

3 tablespoons honey

1 teaspoon lemon juice

2 eating apples, quartered and
   cored

1 banana

1 cup blueberries or seedless
   grapes

Wheat Berry Muësli

Soak wheat berries in ½ cup water at least 12 hours. Soak oatmeal in ½ cup water 30 minutes. Drain wheat and oatmeal, reserving liquid for soup or gravy.

In a large bowl, combine yogurt, honey, and lemon juice. Grate apple quarters, including the peel, and slice banana into yogurt mixture, stirring often to mix in the fruit and to keep it from discoloring.

Stir wheat and oatmeal into the fruit mixture, add berries or grapes, and serve immediately.

Yields about 3 cups

Sprouted Wheat

1. Measure the grains and wash them thoroughly. Begin the sprouting process by soaking the grains in a 1-quart jar of warm water (70° to 80°F) at a ratio of 1 to 4, grain to water, for about 8 to 12 hours. Put the soaking grains in a dark, warm place — under the sink, in the oven, or in a drawer. After soaking the grains, pour off the water.

2. Rinse the soaked grain in a strainer or colander or in the jar, straining the water through cheesecloth. Stretch the cheesecloth over the top of the jar, holding it in place with a rubber band. Air and water, but no grain, should be able to pass freely. Return the jar to the dark, warm place, resting it on its side.

3. Sprouts should be rinsed at least twice a day. To rinse the sprouts, simply fill the jar with water, swish it around briskly, then drain it thoroughly. The sprouts are ready to be used in 3 to 5 days.

Turkey-Bulgur Casserole

1¼ cups bulgur

2 cups turkey gravy or make sauce of:

2 tablespoons butter

4 tablespoons whole wheat flour

2 cups turkey stock

pepper to taste

3 cups diced cooked turkey

2 tablespoons chopped parsley or celery tops

1 teaspoon chopped chives

1 tablespoon butter

1 cup sliced mushrooms

Cook bulgur according to preferred method (see Index).

If making sauce, heat butter in medium-size saucepan. Add flour, stirring to blend it in well. Add stock and stir until sauce is thickened and smooth. Season to taste.

Preheat oven to 325°F. Place turkey pieces in bottom of an oiled ovenproof casserole. Top with parsley or celery tops and chives. In a small saucepan, heat butter and saute mushrooms 5 minutes. Spread mushrooms over turkey and cover with gravy or sauce. Top with bulgur and bake about 25 minutes, or until heated through.

Serves 6

2 tablespoons oil

1 tablespoon chopped onions

1 cup bulgur

2 cups water or chicken stock

dash of pepper

chopped parsley for garnish

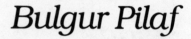

Bulgur Pilaf

Put oil in large skillet; add onions and saute until almost tender (about 8 minutes). Add bulgur and cook until golden.

Add water or chicken stock and pepper. Cover and bring to a boil; reduce heat and simmer 15 minutes. Garnish with parsley and serve.

Serves 4

Savory Steamed Couscous

Bulgur has many culinary roles. It stars in a classic Middle Eastern dish, *couscous*, a delicately flavored base for a stew, usually of lamb or chicken, that has been simmered with onions and seasoned with herbs. Traditionally, the couscous is cooked right above the simmering stew, picking up all the delicious flavors as they rise with the steam. To do this, simply place the bulgur couscous in a steamer or strainer lined with a thick layer of cheesecloth and set to cook inside the tightly covered stewpot.

Tabouli Salad

4 cups boiling water

1¼ cups bulgur

¼ cup navy beans, cooked

¾ cup chopped scallions or onions

3 tomatoes, chopped

1½ cups chopped parsley

1 cucumber, chopped

½ cup lemon juice

¼ cup oil

¼ teaspoon pepper

*P*our boiling water over bulgur and let stand 1 hour, until the grain is light and fluffy. Drain and press out excess water. Add cooked navy beans and all remaining ingredients and chill about 1 hour. Serve on salad greens.

Serves 8

7½ cups whole wheat flour

6 teaspoons dry yeast

1 cup lukewarm water

1 tablespoon honey

4 tablespoons molasses

1 cup warm water

2 cups warm water
(approximately)

No-Knead Whole Wheat Bread
from County Cork, Ireland

*P*lace flour in a large bowl and set it in a warm oven about 20 minutes, to warm flour and bowl. If it is a gas oven, the pilot light will give sufficient heat; if electric, set at lowest temperature.

Dissolve yeast in lukewarm water and add honey.

Mix molasses with 1 cup warm water.

Combine yeast mixture with molasses mixture and add to warmed flour. Add enough water to make a sticky dough (about 2 cups).

Oil 2 large loaf pans, at least 9 × 5 × 3-inches or larger, or 3 small loaf pans and put entire mixture directly into pans. No kneading is involved. Let rise 1 hour. Meanwhile, preheat oven to 400°F.

Bake 30 to 40 minutes, or until crust is brown. Remove pans from oven and leave to cool on racks 10 minutes. Remove loaves from pans and continue to cool on racks before slicing.

Makes 2 large or 3 small loaves

Wheat Germ Muffins

1½ tablespoons dry yeast

½ cup warm water

3 cups wheat germ

4 cups brown rice flour

1 cup skim milk powder

1 cup sesame seeds

1 cup whole wheat flour (or ½ cup whole wheat and ½ cup soy flour)

¾ cup oil

½ cup honey

4½ cups warm water

3 eggs

*P*reheat oven to 400°F.

Dissolve yeast in ½ cup warm water and let stand until dissolved.

In a large bowl, mix wheat germ, rice flour, powdered milk, sesame seeds, and whole wheat flour. In another bowl, mix oil, honey, and 4½ cups warm water.

Slightly beat eggs and add to yeast. Add oil, honey, and water mixture to yeast. Combine the liquid with the dry ingredients. Let stand about 10 minutes, then mix about 1 minute.

Fill well-greased muffin tins with batter. Let stand 10 more minutes. Bake 20 minutes at 400°F; then lower heat to 350°F and bake 5 more minutes.

Makes 30 muffins

2 cups warm water

1 teaspoon diastatic malt

2 tablespoons dry yeast

2 tablespoons oil

5 cups whole wheat flour

Makes 2 medium-size loaves

Whole Wheat and Malt Bread

Combine first 3 ingredients and let sit until bubbly.

Add oil and enough flour to make a soft dough. Knead until smooth and elastic. Put dough in a greased bowl in a warm place to rise until doubled in volume.

Punch down dough, knead briefly, and let rise a second time.

Punch down, divide dough into 2 pieces, and let rest, covered, 10 minutes. Then form into loaves and place in 2 medium-size greased loaf pans. Let rise until dough is about 1½ times the original volume.

Preheat oven to 350°F and bake 35 to 40 minutes, or until loaf sounds hollow when rapped. Cool on wire racks.

Diastatic Malt — Wheat Flour from Sprouts

Sprouts made from wheat are very sweet, because the starches in the grain have been converted to simple sugars in the process of sprouting. When wheat sprouts are used in breads and pancakes, you will find little need for additional sweetener. Wheat sprouts can be dried or roasted, then ground fine and used to replace some flour in baked products.

To make flour from wheat sprouts, dry the sprouts in a very low oven for about 8 hours. The pilot light may suffice if the oven is gas, or if you have an electric oven, the heat of an electric bulb should work. When they are dry, run the sprouts through a seed mill or a blender. This is known as diastatic malt, the unknown factor of the good-tasting breads baked in Europe. It can be used in a blend with unsprouted wheat flour in the ration of 1 to 4. The malt can also be used as a natural sweetener for baked products.

1 cup whole wheat pastry flour

1 cup brown rice flour

3 tablespoons oil

4 tablespoons butter

5 tablespoons ice water

½ cup honey

1 teaspoon cinnamon

2 tablespoons whole wheat flour (not pastry flour)

1 teaspoon grated lemon rind

6 cups peeled, cored, and sliced apples

Apple Pie
with Whole Wheat and Rice Pastry

Sift flours together. Using fingertips, work in oil and then butter until mixture resembles coarse crumbs. Add ice water gradually, kneading slightly to form a ball of dough. Roll out half of dough between sheets of wax paper and press into a 9-inch pie plate.

Combine honey, cinnamon, 2 tablespoons whole wheat flour, and lemon rind and drizzle one-third of mixture onto bottom of pie shell. Pack apple slices into shell and drizzle remaining honey mixture over the top.

Preheat oven to 425°F. Roll out top crust between sheets of wax paper and cover apples, joining top and bottom crusts and fluting the edges. Cut several slits in top crust for steam to escape.

Bake 50 minutes, or until apples are tender. Cool and serve.

Makes 1 9-inch pie

Crepes:

4 eggs

1 tablespoon honey

2 tablespoons melted butter

1 cup milk

1 cup water

1¾ cups whole wheat pastry flour

Sauce:

¾ cup butter

¾ cup honey

¾ cup orange juice

*Crepes
Suzette*

*T*o make crepes, combine ingredients in an electric blender and process until batter is smooth. Let rest 2 hours to allow particles of flour to expand in liquid, resulting in a tender crepe. Just before cooking crepes, process batter again briefly to blend ingredients.

To make the sauce, heat butter, honey, and orange juice together just until they blend well. When ready to serve dessert, dip both sides of each crepe in the orange sauce, fold in half and then in half again and arrange on individual plates. Serve immediately.

Makes 16 8-inch crepes

Standard Method for Cooking Crepes

Heat a heavy skillet or crepe pan to medium-high heat. The pan is ready when a drop of water "dances" on it. Oil pan well, stir batter, then pour it into pan (¼ cup batter will make about the right size crepe). Add more liquid, if necessary, to make a thin crepe. Let crepe cook about 2 minutes. It should be golden brown underneath and dry on top. Flip crepe over, using fingers, and let second side brown for about 1 minute. Slide crepe onto heatproof plate and keep warm in low oven until ready to fill and serve. Crepes may be stacked on top of each other.

Index